NATIVE AMERICAN HOMES

Lincoln James

New York

Published in 2009 by The Rosen Publishing Group, Inc.
29 East 21st Street, New York, NY 10010

Copyright © 2009 by The Rosen Publishing Group, Inc.

Book Design: Haley Wilson

Photo Credits: Cover © Ronald Sherwood/Shutterstock; pp. 2–24 (background) © Jennifer Stone/Shutterstock; pp.
5 (pueblo), 18–19 © Zack Frank/Shutterstock; p. 5 (tepees) © Philip Lange/Shutterstock; p. 5 (igloos) © Andrew
Buckin/Shutterstock; pp. 6–7, 8–9 © MPI/Stringer/Hulton Archive/Getty Images; p. 10 © New York State Museum,
Albany; p. 11 http://en.wikipedia.org/wiki/Image: Apache_Wickiup%2C_Edward_Curtis%2C_1903.jpg;
pp. 12–13 courtesy of www.johnhorse.com; pp. 14–15 © David Hiser/Stone/Getty Images; pp. 16–17 ©
George Burba/Shutterstock; p. 19 © Ralph Lee Hopkins/National Geographic/Getty Images; pp. 20–21 ©
Bryan Brazil/Shutterstock.

ISBN: 978-1-4358-0127-1
6-pack ISBN: 978-1-4358-0128-8

Manufactured in the United States of America

CONTENTS

HOME SWEET HOME

Before Europeans arrived, Native Americans with different **cultures** and **traditions** lived all over North America. They built many different styles of homes depending on what they could find in their surroundings. Some used wood and tree bark. Others used mud and clay. Others dug their homes out of earth or stone. Some even used ice!

Native Americans' homes can tell us a lot about their cultures and ways of life. What do you think you'll learn about Native Americans by studying their homes?

Here are three kinds of Native American homes.
How are they different? How are they the same?

Many people picture a tepee (also spelled "tipi") when they think about Native American homes. Tepees are cone-shaped homes built mainly by tribes of the Great Plains. Tall poles made from **saplings** were used to form the cone shape. Animal skins or tree bark were then wrapped around the frame made by the poles to form the tepee.

Tepees were warm in winter, cool in summer, and dry when it rained. They could be easily taken down and put up again when a tribe moved to a new place.

The Iroquois first built a frame of wooden poles. The poles were bent to make arches for the roof. Beds and shelves were built into the frame. The finished frame was covered with bark, long grasses, and sometimes animal skins. Longhouses had one door on each end and no windows. Roof openings allowed smoke from fires to escape.

CHICKEES

Some Native Americans, such as the Seminole of Florida, built wooden homes called chickees. Chickees had **thatched** roofs and no walls. This kept people cool in hot weather. Animal skins were wrapped around a chickee to make walls when it rained.

The Seminole lived where the ground was wet most of the year. Chickees were built on raised **platforms** to keep people dry and safe from animals such as snakes. Short wooden ladders were used to climb in and out of chickees.

Some tribes made separate chickees for sleeping,
cooking, and eating.

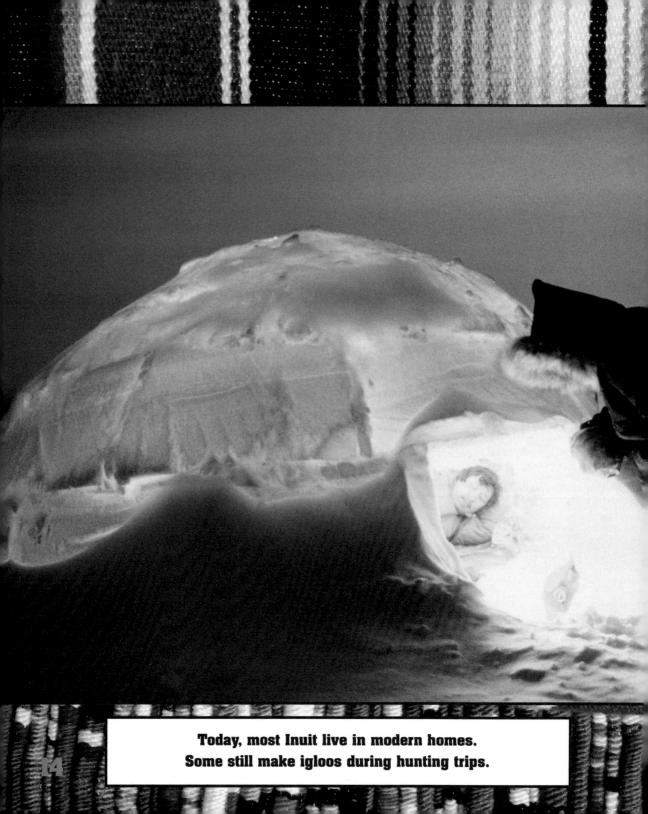

Today, most Inuit live in modern homes.
Some still make igloos during hunting trips.

IGLOOS

The Inuit (IH-noo-wuht) lived where it was cold for most of the year. They used snow and ice to build homes called igloos. An igloo is made of layers of ice cut into blocks. Igloos usually have dome-shaped roofs. They could hold one or two families.

Living in a house made of snow and ice might sound like a cold way to live. However, a well-made igloo keeps out the cold and wind. Even when it's −50ºF (−45.5ºC) outside, it could be as warm as 60ºF (15.5ºC) inside an igloo!

EARTH LODGES

Different Native American groups across North America made their homes by digging living spaces out of the earth. This type of home is called an earth **lodge**. Some Native Americans lived in earth mounds covered by a dome of wood and long grasses.

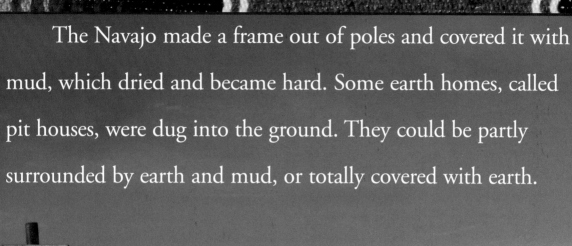

The Navajo made a frame out of poles and covered it with mud, which dried and became hard. Some earth homes, called pit houses, were dug into the ground. They could be partly surrounded by earth and mud, or totally covered with earth.

This Navajo earth lodge is called a hogan.

PUEBLOS

Native Americans of the southwest United States once lived in homes made of bricks called adobe (uh-DOH-bee). Adobe is made by mixing sand, clay, water, and straw. The mixture is packed into **molds** and dried in the sun. Adobe is very strong and lasts a long time.

Adobe and stone blocks were used to build homes called pueblos, many of which are still standing. Pueblos were often built in long, connected rows. Some had more than 100 rooms. A log frame was placed across the top of a pueblo to help support an adobe roof.

MAKING A PUEBLO

mix sand, clay, water, and straw to form a paste

pack the paste into brick molds, then remove molds

allow adobe to bake in sun for a few days

stack dried bricks to form walls

use adobe paste to fill spaces between bricks

cover finished wall with more adobe paste and let dry

build a log frame across the top of the adobe walls

cover log frame with more adobe and let dry

The Spanish called these buildings and the people who built them "pueblos," which comes from the Spanish word for "village."

CLIFF DWELLINGS

Some Native Americans used stone blocks and wood to build their homes and villages high on a tall cliff. Today, these homes are often called cliff **dwellings**. Cliff Palace is the largest cliff dwelling in North America. It's located in Mesa Verde National Park in Colorado.

Cliff Palace has about 150 rooms, but scientists think that only about thirty of the rooms were used for living. The rest were used for storage and special **ceremonies**. Today, you can take a guided tour of Cliff Palace.

Cliff Palace was built around 1200. The people who lived there left around 1300, but no one knows why.

NATIVE AMERICAN HOMES

This chart shows the types of things used to build different Native American homes. Were any of them used to make your home?

	wood/bark	grass/plants	animal skins	snow/ice	dirt/clay	stone
tepee	X		X			
wigwam	X	X	X			
longhouse	X	X	X			
chickee	X	X	X			
igloo				X		
earth lodge	X	X			X	
pueblo	X	X			X	X
cliff dwelling	X					X